D1371846

First Printing, 2018
Wild Cabbage Books
wildcabbagebooks.com

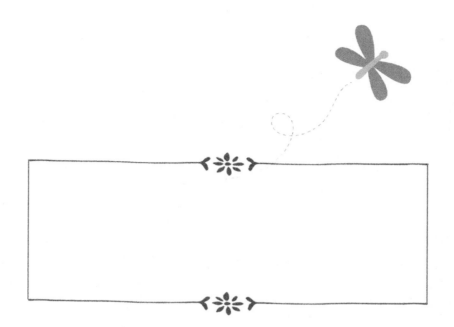

Each of us is limitless; each of us with his
or her right upon the earth.

– Walt Whitman

This above all: to thine ownself be true.

- Shakespeare

In case no one told you today –
You are LLamazing!

No act of kindness, no matter how small, is
ever wasted.

– Aesop

LLeave a LLitle sparkle wherever you go.

Be happy for this moment. This
moment is your life.

– Omar Kayyam

Peace is always beautiful.

– Walt Whitman

The greatest mistake you can make in life
is to be continually fearing you will make
one.

— Elbert Hubbard

Bloom where you are planted.

- 1 Corinthians KJV

Made in the USA
Monee, IL
07 November 2019